To Survival 014

The Ultimate A Field Guide medical to Survival for ANY Disaster

DENNIS HOLDEN

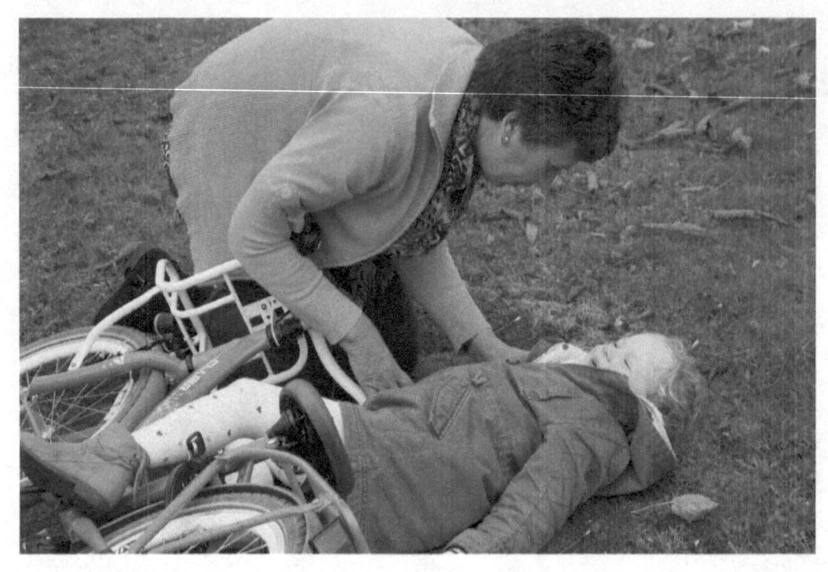

CONTENTS

6.-Rescue Breathing for adults.

-Rescue breathing maneuver

7.-Cardio Pulmonary Resuscitation

- Cardiopulmonary resuscitation maneuver

-Recovery position.

8.-Wounds and hemorrhages.

-Types of wounds and bleeding

-Methods to inhibit a hemorrhage.

9.-Sprains, Dislocations and Fractures.

- Definitions

-Treatment.

10.-Bandages.

Rules for performing a bandage

-Circular bandage

- Herringbone bandage.

-Bandage in.

-Sling.

-Capelin.

11.-Environmental emergencies.

-Heat skin lesions: burns

-Types of burn.

-Specific burns

-Systemic heat injuries: cramp, exhaustion, stroke

   hot.

  - Cold skin lesions: frostbite.

 - Systemic cold injuries: hypothermia.

12.- Most common Medical Conditions in Emergencies

   -Epilepsy and seizures

   -Asthma

  - Acute Myocardial Infarction and angina pectoris

   -Hyperensive crisis

13.-Poisonings and poisonings.

14.-Basic elements of a first aid kit

1.- BASIC DEFINITIONS

FIRST AID:

They are the immediate, temporary and necessary care or help that is given to a person who has suffered an accident, illness or exacerbation of this until the arrival of a doctor or paramedic professional who will take care, only if necessary, of the transfer to a hospital trying to improve or maintain the conditions it is in.

FIRST RESPONDENT:

The first respondent is the first person who decides to participate in the care of an injured person. He may or may not be a healthcare professional. He is in charge of evaluating the scene, beginning the review of the injured and activating the emergency medical service, known in the urban media as the Prehospital Emergency Medical Care System or the Metropolitan Emergency Service.

The obligations of the first respondent are:

- Have the first contact with the injured person.
- Ask for help because you cannot always work properly alone.
- Perform the primary evaluation of the patient.
- Request the support of the appropriate emergency forces.
- Clear the airway.
- If necessary, start CPR.
- Give details of the condition or attention to the Emergency services upon arrival.

How quickly the patient receives adequate care is very important. Since of this the magnitude of the damage, and the prognosis of survival or sequelae.

2.-PERSONAL SAFETY:

To provide good care, it is essential to be free of risks, for which various measures are taken to assess the scene where the accident occurred. It is the first action that is carried out and serves to guarantee physical integrity.

There are three safety rules (SSS) to be able to give good care to the person who needs our help:

- Evaluation of the "scene"
- Check the "security"
- Assess the "situation"

It is also important:

- Have personal protective equipment such as gloves, goggles, face masks.
- The rule of the self: «first me, then me and always me», never forget that before helping a patient, one must avoid becoming a victim.

. Avoiding tunnel vision, which consists of limiting the visual field to a tunnel where only the patient is, without evaluating the rest of the scene, compromises the safety of the first respondent, since it prevents them from identifying potential risks to themselves. .

 The evaluation of the scene is carried out with a total panoramic view of the place from bottom to top, from left to right and from front to back. It is observed what may have been thrown, hung, if there are liquids with which it can slip, cables, glass, animals, etc. Hear the passing of vehicles, alarm voices, detonations, etc. SMELL for gas, gasoline, fertilizers, and other potentially harmful substances. In general apply all the senses in search of potential dangers for the rescuer. WHAT HAPPENED? HOW HAPPENED? WHAT CAN HAPPEN?

Once our safety is guaranteed and the scene is evaluated, the situation is evaluated, that is:

- What was the pre-existing situation?

- Do these conditions still exist?

- HOW MANY ARE INJURED? HOW MANY ARE NOT INJURED?

WHICH IS THE MOST SERIOUS?

Once potential dangers have been ruled out, the approach to the injured person proceeds. This is done by approaching the injured person in front of the visual field, first looking for a verbal response by calling her attention by speaking or making noise. If no answer is found, a closer approach should be sought, to evaluate more data on unconsciousness

To get closer to the person there is what is called the safety position, this consists of standing close to the person, leaning on 2 points, we are located at the height of the trunk of our patient, kneeling with one leg at the height of the hip, the which should go with the knee resting on the floor, and the other leg, at the height of the ribs, should be placed in hip and knee flexion, thus making an angle of 90 ° without resting it on the floor.

This position both protects and It keeps us alert to flee if necessary, it also allows an approach to the person who needs our help.

3.- Evaluation of the Injured:

SIMULTANEOUS IMMEDIATE ASSESSMENT.

HOW IS IT DONE?

It is the evaluation in which the general state of the patient, state of consciousness, respiratory and circulatory condition is determined in a period of no more than 10 seconds.

Once in your safe position, the patient is touched on the shoulders and shaken slightly while asking how they are. Sir, sir, are you okay?

State of consciousness is determined by locating it with the ADVI method

A: the person is alert, speaks fluently, stares at the explorer and is aware of what is happening around him.

V: the person presents a verbal response, although he is not alert, he can respond coherently to the questions that are asked, and he responds when called.

D: the person responds only to the application of some painful stimulus, such as firmly pressing some bone protrusion such as the sternum or clavicles; Less harmful examination methods such as lightly brushing your lashes or tapping your finger in the middle of the eyebrows can be used, this will produce an involuntary blink, which is considered a response.

I: the person does not present any of the previous answers, is Unconscious

PRIMARY ASSESSMENT

It is the initial evaluation that helps us identify the injuries or conditions that can endanger the life of the patient. It must be fast and effective. And it applies to patients in whom unconsciousness has been demonstrated

To carry out this evaluation, the ABC mnemonic is used.

A: "Airway" open airway and cervical control.

B: "breath" ventilation.

C: "circulation" circulation and hemorrhage control.

A: That the airway is open and without risk of obstruction. The mouth is opened in search of something that could obstruct the airway, if there is something within our reach we remove it by making a hook sweep with the index finger, if there is nothing we will do the head tilt technique .

B: It is evaluated whether ventilation is present or not. Mnemonics are used:

See: the patient›s chest (if it rises and falls).

Listen: breathing

Feel: the air that comes out of the mouth or nose

It is necessary to determine if it breathes by itself, how often and how deep the breaths are.

C: The presence of signs of circulation is determined, such as the pulse or the coloration of the skin, if it is pale, bluish; body temperature. And check for any obvious bleeding.

SECONDARY ASSESSMENT:

Injuries are identified that by themselves do not endanger the life of our patient, but that in addition to each other, they do. Look for deformities, subsidence, asymmetry, hemorrhages, crackles, etc.

The evaluation is performed by palpating from head to toe starting with the head, neck, thorax, abdomen, hips, legs, feet, arms and spine.

4.- VITAL SIGNS:

They are the physiological signals that indicate the presence of life of a person. These are data that we can collect on our own with or without the help of a team. The vital signs are:

- Respiratory rate: number of breaths per minute.
- Heart rate: number of heart beats per minute.
- Pulse: reflex of the heartbeat in the distal area of the body.
- Blood Pressure: the force with which the heart beats.
- Body temperature of the patient.
- Capillary filling.
- Pupillary reflex

- Respiratory rate: as in the primary evaluation, it is taken using the VES mnemonics (see, hear, feel), counting how many ventilation\e bbn nnns the person gives per minute. This is the only vital sign that one can control oneself, so it is important not to tell the patient that he is going to be evaluated so that he does not alter his ventilatory pattern.

- Heart rate: it is taken with a stethoscope (or by placing the ear over the mentioned point) which is placed at the level of the fifth intercostal space in the midclavicular line, that is, at the level of the left nipple, inclining it slightly towards the left, like the respiratory rate, it is counted how many times the heart beats in a minute.

- Pulse: this sign indicates that blood is reaching all areas of the body. We must count how many pulsations there are in a minute and detect if it is weak or strong. There are different areas to take a pulse.

The evaluation of these three signs can be abbreviated by counting the beats, beats or breaths in 20 or 30 seconds and multiplying it by 3 or 2 respectively, thus obtaining the total number of beats, beats or breaths per minute, to give us a general idea of the cardiac pattern, circulatory or respiratory. But only in cases of extreme urgency where suggested time is not available.

-Carotid pulse: the index and middle fingers are placed on the chin, followed in a straight line towards the cricoid cartilage (Adam›s apple) and is traversed laterally for approximately ٢cm with some pressure. Stimulating the neck should be avoided because a nerve passes in this area which, when stimulated, causes the vital signs of our patient to begin to decrease.

-Radial pulse: the wrist is discovered, with the index and middle fingers the line of the thumb is followed up to the wrist and pressure is exerted towards the bone.

• Blood pressure: the baumanometer is placed on the arm with the arrow or the hoses in the area of the artery (the bend of the elbow), it is closed but not squeezed to the arm , the pulse of the artery that passes in that zone and there the stethoscope bell is placed ; with the knob the needle of the baumanometer is raised to 160mmHg or depending on the pressure normally handled by our patient , then the knob is slowly opened to be able to hear where the heartbeat starts to be heard and where it stops hearing. The first noise and the last noise we hear will tell us which blood pressure.

Technique V.E.S.

It is the fastest and most effective way to detect the presence of vital signs. It is performed once the unconsciousness has been verified, and the working position is acquired (both knees bent resting on the floor, one at the height of the trunk or shoulders and the other at the hip or trunk) It is done by placing the hatred near the face and mouth of the injured, opening the airway, fixing the gaze on the trunk, to distinguish its movement, In order to See, Listen and Feel the breath, the passage of air.

• Pupillary reflex: if you have a small flashlight, shine the beam of light into the eye and observe how the pupil contracts. If you do not have the light-producing element, open the upper eyelid abruptly and observe the same reaction, or with your hand cover the eye and remove it suddenly to see the contraction of the pupil.

• Body temperature: taken by means of a thermometer either under the arm or under the tongue. You can also roughly know the body temperature by feeling the person's skin since it can feel very hot or cold.

5.- OBSTRUCTION OF THE AIRWAY:

There are different risk situations (to present it) such as the ingestion of food or foreign objects as well as bronchial aspiration (that the patient breathes secretions such as blood or vomiting), chronic diseases, anaphylaxis (allergies) or inflammatory processes. All these situations can totally or partially close the airway, preventing the adequate passage of air. Causing respiratory arrest. However, only upper airway obstruction (throat or larynx, and trachea) by solid objects such as food or foreign bodies, can be resolved by the airway clearance maneuver described on the following pages. While in the case that it is the lower airway (small and large caliber bronchi) due to chronic diseases, bronchial aspiration, anaphylaxis, they require specialized medical attention in the hospital.

Respiratory arrest is the sudden interruption of breathing which can produce cardiac arrest in a few minutes due to the relationship between the two systems.

A person who does not receive oxygen between 4 to 6 min. will have neurological damage.

To PREVENT this problem it is important to:
• Do not give or let children play with objects such as buttons, seeds, balloons, or coins.
• Do not allow children to play when they are eating.
• Do not give children foods with shells or bones.
• Prevent children from falling asleep while eating candy or gum. .
• Do not cover children's faces or leave heavy blankets or large pillows within reach.
• And in the case of adults, Do not hold items in their mouths that can be easily swallowed.

The most common causes of respiratory arrest due to airway obstruction are the presence of foreign bodies or anaphylaxis (acute allergic reactions where the trachea and / or throat become swollen and closed) in addition to the drooping of the tongue (main cause death).
The fall of the tongue is observed when the level of consciousness is decreased and there is decreased and there

is depression in the nervous system, for example:

- Post-operative state.
- Acute alcoholism.
- Epilepsy crisis.
- Nervous system depressant medication
- Trauma to skull
- Low sugar (etc).

For its treatment, the CAUSE must be DEFINED

Emergency treatment consists of:

• Define the cause of the obstruction and if it is total (no air enters) or

partial (the person may make some sounds, therefore a little air enters),

• Give the patient confidence (tell him that we are going to help him), if he is not unconscious.

• Activate the SMU

• In the event that the obstruction is partial, you are only asked to cough until the object comes out.

• If the obstruction is total, the airway clearance maneuver should be applied.

• Do not abandon care until the emergency bodies arrive.

TECHNIQUES TO OPEN THE AIRWAY:

There are three techniques that can keep the airway patent in case of unconsciousness, it is important that during the entire treatment we give the patient and until the emergency services arrive, the airway must always be open.

1. Head tilt: one hand is placed on the forehead of the patient in a claw shape pushing it down and the other with two fingers on the chin pushing it up. (contraindicated in cases of trauma)

2. Mandibular traction: the ring and middle fingers are placed at the level of the patient›s jaw and the jaw is pushed forward to open the airway. (Not recommended for the civilian population).

3. Chin lift: the thumb is placed on the upper part of the chin and the other fingers on the lower part to "pinch" it and elevate it. (Not recommended for the civilian population).

To be able to apply this maneuver, the airway must be totally obstructed, in its upper portion. If you hear that the person may cough or emit a whistle or speak with difficulty, all you do is calm the person and insist that they continue coughing.

If the person is holding their hands around their neck and making no sound, you should position yourself on the back of the person with one of your legs between the patient's to prevent them from falling and injuring themselves if they fall unconscious. We surround the person under the armpits with our arms, look for the navel and the tip of the sternum and in the middle of those two points that in thin people are approximately 2 fingers above the navel, our hand is placed in the shape of a fist and the other supporting the first to perform the J-shaped compressions that are necessary for the person to expel the foreign object.

Depending on the size of the person is the force with which the compressions are given. In the case of a pregnant person, compression is done at the thoracic level, two fingers above the xiphoid appendix (point of convergence of the ribs, "the pit of the stomach").

DISOBSTRUCTION MANEUVER IN UNCONSCIOUS PATIENT.

When the person is unconscious, the primary evaluation (ABC) is carried out and if the patient does not breathe, two insufflations are given with the patient›s neck in hyperextension, we fix his head by resting the palm of our hand closest to his forehead; we cover the nose with the thumb and index finger of it, then, covering his mouth with our mouth, we inflate (blow) strongly for \ second. This in order to know if the airway is obstructed, if the air does not pass, we will observe that the thorax does not expand, and we will feel a great resistance to our insufflation, in that case, we reposition and give two more insufflations.
If it is still obstructed, we squat on the hip of the person lying on his back, locate the compression point described above, place the heel of one hand on it with

the fingers extended, while with the other hand, we hug the first, and we give 5 abdominal compressions up and into the chest, at the end of which, we must get up and go to the patient's face, open his mouth and explore in search of the object that obstructed the airway.

If we find it, we proceed to remove it by trapping it with a hooked finger, otherwise, we repeat two insufflations, with replacement in case the air does not pass, to rule out or confirm the persistence of the obstruction; if so, the procedure is repeated. But if the air already passes freely into the airway, we perform a VES, looking for vital signs and thus determine if you are in respiratory or cardiac arrest. If there is no such situation, it is placed in a recovery position.

After these maneuvers, all patients must be medically evaluated, as there are complications that must be ruled out.

6.- BREATH OF SALVATION:

It is applied in case of demonstrating the absence of respiration with an unobstructed airway. (respiratory faliure). Its purpose is to reestablish the normal respiratory pattern, through stimulation of the brain by the expansion and reduction of the thorax.

This is accomplished by blowing air into the chest cavity at the rate that an average adult would normally breathe.

Insufflation is performed with the described technique every 5 seconds, 12 times, thus completing one minute. A good way to keep up is to count:

1,2,3,1 (this number indicates the insufflation being applied), INSUFLO 1,2,3,2, insufflation

1,2,3,3, insufflation

1,2,3,12, insufflation

At the end of this first minute, VES must be performed, we have several options:

A) ventilates (breathes) and has a pulse ...Recovery position, we have saved

B) DOES NOT ventilate (breathe) and has a pulse... Repeat Rescue.

C) DOES NOT ventilate (breathe) or have a pulse... It has

evolved to unemployment cardiorespiratory, we must start CPR

7.- CARDIO PULMONARY RESUSCITATION (CPR):

Cardiorespiratory arrest is the sudden and simultaneous interruption of breathing and the functioning of the heart, due to the relationship that exists between the respiratory and circulatory systems. Respiratory arrest may occur and the heart may continue to function, but cardiac arrest may ensue within a few minutes, when first aid is not provided immediately. When the heart does not function normally, the blood does not circulate, the supply of oxygen to all the cells of the body is reduced, causing damage to other tissues as time passes.

The most common causes of cardiorespiratory arrest are:

- Heart attack.
- Deep hypothermia.
- Shock.
- Head trauma.

-
-
-
-

If an unconscious person is found and when performing the primary evaluation (ABC) it is found that they do not have a pulse and that they are not breathing but that the airway is permeable (air enters), the CPR technique is performed, which is a combination of breaths and chest compressions that give an external cardiac massage.

It should be checked for 10 seconds if the patient is breathing and has a pulse.

If it does not have it, the costal edge is located, following it until the lower point of the sternum is found. Once located, two fingers are placed upwards and then place the heel of your hand with the fingers raised and the other hand hugging it. Compressions should be with the arms straight and perpendicular to the patient's body.

Adults: **30 are made**

CHEST COMPRESSIONS FOR 2 VENTILATIONS AT A RATE OF 100 COMPRESSIONS PER MINUTE UNTIL SIGNS OF CIRCULATION APPEAR.

Whenever maneuvers are given, be it unblocking, rescue breathing or CPR, it is important to say what we are finding in the patient and what we are doing out loud so that if there is someone who knows first aid who listens to us, we can to help.

Recovery position: Once the pulse, breathing and airway have been recovered, the affected person should be placed in a recovery position, which consists of placing the person on their side with one leg bent so that they do not return.

The CPR maneuver is discontinued when:

Hospital or come to help us

Exhausted.

Life (return life).

Paramedics or someone more trained tells us to stop giving it.

8.- WOUNDS AND BLEEDING:

Soft tissue injuries are the most common problems in first aid care, these injuries can cause serious injury, disability or death. A wound is any injury produced by an external or internal agent that involves soft tissue, these can be divided into:

• Open wounds: in which the separation of the soft tissues is observed.

• Closed wounds: in which the separation of the tissues is not observed, the hemorrhage accumulates under the skin, in cavities or in the viscera.

AMONG THE OPEN WOUNDS WE HAVE:

• Sharp wounds: produced by sharp objects such as cans, glass, knives, etc.

• Puncture wounds: They are produced by pointed objects, such as nails, needles, ice picks, etc.

• Puncture wounds: They are produced by pointed and sharp objects, such as scissors, daggers, knives, or a broken bone.

- Lacerations: these are wounds with irregular edges that are not confronted.
- Wounds from a firearm projectile: depending on the type of weapon, the caliber of the bullet and the distance, the wound has different characteristics.
- Abrasions: are wounds caused by friction with rough surfaces, it is what is commonly known as scrapes.
- Avulsions: Are those where the body tissue is separated and torn without completely detaching from the affected part.
- Amputations: is the separation traumatic or pathological ?? of a limb and can be total, partial or glove finger.

The TREATMENT of a wound is as follows:

- Remove clothing covering the wound
- Use latex gloves, to avoid contagion of any disease as well as contaminating the wound.
- It is cleaned with gauze and saline solution or drinking water, removing excess blood and dirt that it may have. The way to clean with the gauze is from the inside out in eccentric circles, starting from the center of the wound, these being bigger and bigger; the gauze is turned over and done again to avoid infecting it.

The procedure is repeated, two or three more times

• Iodine is applied to prevent infection.

• The wound is covered with gauze.

• Do not apply any type of home remedy because they can cause infections.

• Do not apply drugs or antibiotics because we can cause an allergic reaction.

Hemorrhage is the exit of blood from the ducts or vessels through which it circulates, this exit implies a gradual loss of blood which must be controlled as soon as possible so that it does not become complicated.

They are divided into different types:

BY SPACE TO WHICH THE BLOOD IS Poured

• Internal hemorrhages: those in which blood drains into the internal cavities of the body.

• External hemorrhages: in which the blood spills to the outside of the body.

BY ORIGIN

• Arterial hemorrhage: characterized by bright red blood and its rhythmic spurt that matches the heartbeat and pulse.

• Venous hemorrhage:
characterized by a dark red color and a continuous and
uniform blood flow.

• Capillary hemorrhage: it only involves capillaries,
which is why it is scarce and can be easily controlled,
usually a bruise (hematoma) is formed

To COHIBIT BLEEDING you must:

• Locate the precise place of the exit of blood and
the type of hemorrhage for which the area must be
discovered.

• Exert direct pressure on the hemorrhage for 5-10 minutes with a compress. If it fills with blood, do not remove
it but place another compress on top to avoid undoing
the clot that is beginning to form.

• If it doesn't work ...

• Apply indirect pressure to an area between the wound
and the

Heart, for example, if the bleeding is in a hand, it can be
pressed on the location of the brachial pulse, this to prevent the passage of blood towards the wound that conditions the hemorrhage, thus preventing it from being lost.

• If it doesn't work ...

- Elevate the affected part above the level of the heart so that the bleeding gradually slows down.
- As a last resort...
- Place ice wrapped in a clean cloth or bag around the affected area to prevent bleeding. (cryotherapy)
- But always ...
- Apply a moderate compression bandage

The tourniquet is contraindicated in most cases, only in amputations is this technique used and as follows:

- A wide bandage or canvas (not less than 5cm) is placed 4 fingers from the wound.
- Two turns around the limb
- A simple knot is made and a rod, pencil, etc. is placed on the knot and two more knots are made on it.
- Turns slowly until the bleeding stops.
- It must be released and retightened every 5 min.
- Immediately transfer the person to the hospital.

If the bleeding is internal or it is suspected that the person may have a hemorrhage due to the injury they had, they should be transferred as quickly as possible.

In the case of embedded objects, it MUST NOT BE REMOVED because it may cause further injury in addition to causing greater bleeding, the object must be reduced as much as possible and immobilized in the place where it is, indirect pressure is exerted and is transferred.

If the impaled object is in the eye, it is also recommended to bandage the other eye to prevent the eyes from moving and further injury.

9.- SPRAINS, DISLOCATIONS AND FRACTURES:

• Sprain: it is the momentary separation of the articular surfaces causing the total or partial injury or rupture of the articular ligaments. When there is a major ligament tear, the edges of the joint can be separated in gentle movements.

• Luxation: It is the persistent displacement of an articular surface outside the cavity or space that contains it, causing loss of contact between the bones of the joint, which is known as dislocation

The propensity to a sprain or dislocation is due to the structure of the joints as well as the condition of the person, strength of the muscles and tendons that surround it. These are caused by rapid movements where the joint is forced too much in one of its normal movements or makes an abnormal movement.

The Signs and Symptoms of a sprain or dislocation are.

Redness in the affected area.

Intense pain.

Lump or inflammation in the affected area.

Heat, the affected area feels hot. Progressive functional disability.

Hypersensitivity in the area.

In the case of dislocation, there is a loss of morphology and the absence of normal bone protrusions. Or presence of abnormal bone margins Treatment.

• Rest the affected joint.

• Cool the area to prevent possible bleeding and reduce inflammation. No

• Immobilize the affected limb, preventing the area from bearing weight.

• If possible, slight elevation of the affected part

• Do not apply massages or apply ointments or ointments.

- Fracture: is the loss of continuity of bone tissue, either total or partial. Caused by direct trauma, that is, a direct blow that breaks the area where it is made or by indirect trauma where the bone is fractured due to the forces transmitted along it from the point of impact; or by sudden twisting.

With a fracture, there is usually damage and injury to the surrounding soft tissues.

Fractures are injuries that by themselves are not life-threatening, but if not properly cared for, they can get worse and can cause including the death of the patient, if these are accompanied by arterial hemorrhages or if they compromise the nervous system.

They are divided into:

- Closed fractures: in which the bone does not come out through the skin
- Open fractures: where the bone comes out and breaks the skin producing an open wound which implies visible bleeding.
- Fissure: it is a slight fracture where the bone undergoes a partial fracture without the edges separating completely.

• Green branch fracture: this occurs mainly in children because their bones are not yet completely calcified, the bone does not break completely

The Signs and Symptoms are:
Redness in the affected area.
Intense pain.
Lump or inflammation in the affected area.
Heat, the affected area feels hot.
Deformity of the area. Crepitus of the affected area. Loss of functionality.

TREATMENT:
• Do not move the patient.
• If there is bleeding, inhibit it by indirect pressure and cryotherapy in addition to covering the wound with a gauze, dressing or clean cloth.
• Do not try to accommodate the broken bone
• Immobilize the fracture in the position it is in to avoid further pain and aggravate the injury.

10.- BANDAGES.

Bandages are procedures made with strips of canvas or

other materials, in order to wrap an injured limb or other parts of the human body. Are used mainly in wounds, hemorrhages, fractures, sprains, dislocations, fixation of dressings, splints and give support to joints.

• The bandage should be placed with the roll of the bandage out of the area to be bandaged.
• Before starting any bandage, two safety turns should be given so that it does not run.
• It should be started from the distal or furthest part of the heart to the closest to avoid the accumulation of blood.
• When a joint is going to be bandaged to give it support, the bandage is started from the part proximal or closest to the heart to the farthest to prevent it from running.
• Whenever we are going to immobilize an area due to an injury, it is done including the nearby joints to avoid more damage and give it support.
• If possible avoid bandaging the fingers and toes

-Circular or spiral bandage:
It is used to fix the beginning and end of an

immobilization or to fix a dressing or splint,
Two safety turns are made and the bandage continues to rotate in the
same direction towards the upper part of the limb ensuring that the turns are the same size.

Herringbone bandage: It is used to put pressure on a certain area (inhibit bleeding).
It begins as the circular bandage but instead of going up all the time, one turn up and one down is interspersed, forming a series of «Xs» as you go forward, ensuring that the line formed by the crosses remains straight to exercise pressure on that area.

-Bandage in eight or turtle:
It is used in the joints (ankle, knee, shoulder, elbow, wrist), since it allows a certain mobility.
The joint is placed slightly flexed. The bandage is directed alternately upwards and then downwards, so that at the back the bandage always passes and crosses in the center of the joint. Depending on the movement we want to avoid is the area where the cross of the bandage will be placed.

Sling: It is used to support the hand, arm or forearm in case of wounds, burns, fractures, sprains and dislocations. Two safety turns are made on the affected arm and the bandage is placed towards the hand and then towards the neck in such a way that the neck is the one that carries the weight of the limb.
Position the victim's forearm slightly obliquely, meaning that the hand is higher than the elbow.

-Bandage for the head or capeline: It begins by making two circular safety turns horizontally around the head. Then the bandage is directed by means of folds that cover the entire cranial vault, since it is covered, two horizontal turns are made to fix all the folds of the bandage (it is done between two people).
For the immobilization of a fractured limb, magazines, pillows, cardboard, wood, splints, another part of the body such as the leg or another finger, etc. can be used. As long as it prevents movement of the affected limb.

11.- ENVIRONMENTAL EMERGENCIES:

It includes a wide range of different injuries and conditions divided into two main categories: hot and cold.

Each of these is in turn divided into localized (skin) conditions such as burns or injuries caused by cold, and systemic conditions such as hyperthermia or hypothermia.

SKIN INJURIES FROM HEAT:

-Burns: A burn is the damage or destruction of the skin or deeper tissues such as muscle and bone by heat or cold produced by external agents, whether physical, chemical, electrical and / or any of their combinations. Causes sudden, life-threatening dehydration.

• Physical agents: hot solids (plates, stoves), liquids (oil or water), sun, cold, etc.
• Chemical agents: acids (a. Hydrochloric, sulfuric, muriatic, etc) and alkalis (caustic soda)
• Electrical agents: electrical discharges at different voltages.

SEVERITY is determined according to:
• Depth.
•Extension.
• Body region.
• Inhalation injury.

Serious burns are those that make it difficult to breathe, those that cover more than one part of the body or that are found on the head, neck, hands, feet or genitals, deep burns or those caused by chemical substances, explosions or electricity.

They are classified into:
• 1st degree burns: They affect the most superficial layer of the skin, which heals spontaneously in 3 to 5 days and does not produce sequelae. It is usually caused by long exposure to the sun, a campfire, etc. Symptoms are redness of the skin, dry skin, pain
intense burning type and moderate inflammation.

• 2nd degree burns: affects the second layer of the skin causing blisters, blisters or blisters, inflammation of the area and a pink or bright red color and pain.
3rd degree burns: affects all the skin, muscles, tendons, nerves and bone, charred white color is observed, the skin loses elasticity and does not regenerate and there is no pain due to the destruction of the nerve endings. This type of burn is caused by prolonged contact with hot, caustic or electrical elements.

The general TREATMENT is:

- Reassure the patient.
- Remove clothing that is not stuck.
- Irrigate with plenty of clean water to cool the burn.
- Cover the wound with a moist sterile dressing, removing excess water.
- Cover this dressing with a clean, dry cloth.
- Prevent hypothermia by keeping in a warm environment.
- Do not burst ampules or blisters.
- Do not apply ointments or ointments.
- Administer plenty of fluids by mouth as long as the victim is conscious.
- Immediate transfer to the specialized center.

- Burns due to the inhalation of vapors: When there is inhalation of vapors, they generally cause burns of the airways.
respiratory systems, so it is essential to assess whether the person can breathe on their own and if they have a pulse, in case they are absent, start CPR.
- Burns from fire: If the person is running, stop him, lay him on the ground, put out the victim's fire with a

blanket, water or sand, avoiding the extinguisher because it is very corrosive and toxic.

Chemical burns: The burned area (eyes, skin or mucous membranes) should be washed with plenty of running water for no less than 30 minutes. (Warning: some chemicals react with water, check manuals specialized in handling chemicals).

• Electric burns: Electric burns are almost always third degree, with an entry site and one or more exit sites, where you can see charred and explosion areas, they generally do not bleed and are painless, the most important injuries are internal.

Before caring for a person with this type of burns you should:

• Interrupt contact with the current and / or cut off the electrical supply.

• Stand on a dry rubber or wooden surface.

• Remove the electrical source with a wooden object. DO NOT touch with your hands.

• Assess respiration and pulse; if they are not present, initiate CPR.

• Transfer as quickly as possible to a Hospital.

SYSTEMIC HEAT INJURIES:

Heat Cramp: Occurs when exercising or doing heavy work in hot weather without proper rehydration. There is pain, muscle stiffness on palpation, and functional limitation.

The treatment is:
- Remove the patient from the hot environment.
- Gently stretch the muscle.
- Give massage to promote circulation
- Administer fluids with electrolytes such as sports drinks or Vida Oral Serum

Heat exhaustion: It is a consequence of the excessive loss of fluids and electrolytes with the absence of adequate replacement due to exposure to high ambient temperatures. The characteristic signs of this condition are nausea, slight dizziness, anxiety, headache, red, cold and sweaty skin.
The treatment to follow is:
- Remove the patient to a cool place.
- Administration of fluids (electrolytes)

- Remove excess clothing.
- Assess whether it requires a transfer.

Heat stroke: It is the sudden loss of the body's ability to control internal heat dissipation which can be caused by prolonged exposure to high temperatures or by physical activities under the same conditions. The characteristic symptoms are: red and hot skin, sweating, anxiety, headache, seizures, high temperature (above 40°C)

The treatment to follow is:
- Cooling the patient by means of compresses of warm or cold water.
- Administer fluids orally
- Transfer.

COLD SKIN INJURIES:

Frostbite: It is the freezing of body tissues as a consequence of exposure to very cold temperatures that occurs mainly in isolated areas such as hands, feet, face and ears.

The treatment to follow is:

- Place the patient in a warm environment.
- Place the affected body part on a hot surface.
- Warm up to body temperature.
- If the lesion is deep, rewarming is not recommended.
- Avoid giving massages

SYSTEMIC INJURIES FROM COLD:

Hypothermia: It is the condition in which the internal body temperature falls below 35ºC, affects healthy individuals who, not being prepared for it, are exposed to adverse conditions, or can develop secondary to the patient's disease or pre-existing injury.

The survival of the patient depends on the age, the time of submergence or exposure, how much the body temperature drops, in case of

The most common causes are:

- Staying outdoors during winter without protecting yourself.
- Falling from a boat in cold water.
- Wear wet clothes for a long time when it is windy or cold.

Exerting strenuous exertion or ingesting insufficient food or drink in cold weather, even in temperatures above freezing.

Symptoms usually start slowly. As the person develops hypothermia, their thinking and moving skills are often slowly lost.

The treatment to follow is:

• Prevent heat loss by taking the person to a warm place and covering with warm blankets.

• Assess if the person can breathe and has a pulse, if not present, start CPR

• Careful mobilization of the patient.

• Remove wet clothing.

• Give warm sweet liquids by mouth

• Avoid heating and massaging the extremities.

• It should not be assumed that a person who is lying motionless in the cold is dead, one can only know that he is dead when it is at room temperature.

• Alcohol should not be given to the victim.

12.- Most common medical conditions in the emergency room:

SEIZURES AND EPILEPSY:

A seizure occurs when the brain stops working normally due to injury, illness, fever or infection, the electrical activity of the brain becomes irregular. This can cause loss of body control leading to seizures. The most common causes of a seizure are epilepsy and diseases such as rabies and tetanus, head injuries, poisoning, high fevers, etc.

A seizure is characterized primarily by generalized muscle contractions in the extremities and face.

Epilepsy is a chronic disease characterized by repeated seizures, more or less spaced in time, called epileptic seizures, due to an excessive discharge of brain neurons.

The symptoms of epilepsy vary depending on the different types of epileptic diseases that exist, from a small alteration of sensitivity in an area of the body or movements similar to a tic disorder, the most important being the so-called generalized grand mal or tonic crisis. clonic

characterized by:

• Loss of consciousness and falls to the ground, abruptly

• Involuntary contractions of large muscle groups, it can

be an entire limb, followed by sudden relaxation and later a new contraction, I take this in an uncontrolled and un-stoppable rhythm.

• Many patients before the loss of consciousness have sensations that warn them of what is going to happen, called "aura", such as the subjective perception (only the person feels them) of smells, colors or sounds (smell of almonds, little lights , buzzing, etc)

• At the end of the movements the patient enters a kind of coma or stuporous state, they wake up without re-membering what happened, they have severe headaches and whole body pain, manifesting to be very exhausted. The treatment to follow is:

• Remove any object that could injure the patient.

• Stay away while you are having a seizure.

• Place a soft, large, padded object that cannot pass into the throat, which serves as a teether to avoid dropping the tongue or amputation of it, before it begins to con-vulse.

Not during, as it can be harmful to the first respondent.

• In the past loosen clothing and prevent bites.

• Do not hold it.

- Do not try to open your mouth at the time of the seizure.
- At the end of a seizure monitor vital signs
- Prevent hypothermia
- Place in recovery position

- Transfer to the nearest hospital.

It occurs when the sugar levels in the body are below normal values (70-110 gr / dL), generally caused by not being able to compensate for the excessive consumption of sugar without adequate replacement, or by the inability to metabolize it properly as in the case of Diabetes.

Some of the common causes are lack of food, end-stage pregnancy, severe malnutrition, reduced caloric intake, excess insulin production, excess fasting insulin administration, etc.

The most frequent symptoms are: fatigue, headache, hunger, dizziness, decreased consciousness, salivation and even unconsciousness.

Its treatment is:

• Measurement of blood glucose by means of a finger blood sample that is placed on test strips (dextrostix) or on the glucometer

• Identify the cause of low blood sugar.

• Administer sweet liquids.

•Transfer to the hospital.

ASTHMA

It is a pulmonary disease characterized by episodes of sudden and sustained contraction of the bronchi, manifested mainly by pulmonary wheezing (whistling) perceptible on inspiration or expiration, of variable dimension, it is produced by inflammation of the airways causing difficulty in between the air flow to the lungs. It can be triggered by some type of allergy to physical factors or medications, by prolonged physical activities and usually begins suddenly.

The general treatment is:

• Reassure the person.

• Have the bronchodilator on hand and check that it works by firing it into the air.

• Ask the person to breathe out.

• At the moment you are going to inhale, trigger the discharge of the bronchodilator in your mouth. Up to 3 shots can be fired in a period of 2.5 hours.

ACUTE MYOCARDIAL INFARCTION AND ANGINA PEAK:

Angina is a type of chest pain related to the heart that occurs due to insufficient supply of blood and oxygen to this organ. The pain of angina can be similar to that seen in a heart attack and is called stable angina when chest pain begins at a predictable level of activity (for example, going up a steep hill), usually subsides with rest within 5 minutes . However, if the pain occurs unexpectedly after light activity or occurs at rest, it is called unstable angina. Or lasts more than 10 minutes without giving in to rest

While the acute myocardial infarction is the death of cardiac tissue caused by a coronary obstruction.

These two conditions are characterized by anxiety and restlessness, sweating, paleness, nausea, vomiting, crushing pain in the chest, high respiratory rate, the pain can radiate to the neck, left arm and abdomen.

The difference between the two conditions is that in acute infarction the pain increases while in angina pectoris with rest it begins to decrease.

In both cases the treatment is:

• Reassure the patient because usually any chest pain is related to a heart attack

• Applying medication if it has not been taken is not recommended if its management is unknown.

• Transfer to the hospital

• Vital signs monitoring

HYPERTENSIVE CRISIS

ARTERIAL HYPERTENSION: It is considered arterial hypertension when the value is higher than 140/90 mmHg, causing hemodynamic problems such as poor circulation of small vessels or rupture of the same, which is favorable in people over 35 years of age. This is due to excessive physical efforts, coronary problems or lack of

elasticity in veins and arteries, the risk factors are:

• Middle age or older

• Being overweight or obese

- Taking Contraceptives
- Mellitus diabetes
- Family inheritance of cardiovascular disease
- Male gender
- Stress
- Smoking

Hypertension occurs during its initial stage without symptoms, silently, affecting vital organs such as the heart, brain, kidneys, eyes and arteries while in a late stage it can cause:

- Prolonged and repetitive headache
- Drowsiness, confusion and dizziness
- Numbness and tingling of the hands and feet
- Nosebleeds with no apparent cause
- Fatigue and tiredness
- Injected eyes (eye spills)
- Reddish skin.
- Insomnia.

Usually, chronic cases do not warrant emergency treatment, unless the increase in blood pressure causes fainting, severe headache, blurred vision, a feeling of tightness in the chest, etc.

Which are signs of the condition known as Hypertensive Crisis, which, depending on the magnitude, puts life and or the function of organs such as the kidneys, brain and heart at risk.

Treatment for hypertensive crisis is:

• Calm the patient.

• Place him lying down with the thorax at 45°

• Loosen clothing

• Vital signs monitoring

• Transfer to the hospital

13.- POISONING AND POISONING:

Toxic is the synthetic substance capable of endangering health or causing death by accidentally entering the body, while the Natural toxin that can be produced by some plants or animals is considered a poison.

Poisoning is the body's reaction to the entry of a poison which can cause injury or even death depending on the type of poison, assimilated dose, concentration, route of administration, etc.

According to the route of exposure they can be divided into:

- Inhaled (by respiratory route)
- Absorbed (dermally)
- Ingested (by digestive route)
- Injected.

Depending on the dose and route of management the signs and symptoms that the person may present are.

- Eye irritation.
- Altered state of consciousness OR UNCONSCIOUS-NESS
- Lack of oxygen.
- Nausea, dizziness and vomiting
- Headache.
- Seizures.
- BLUE coloration of the lips or burns in the corners of the nose and mouth.
- Evidence of an insect or animal bite.

The treatment to follow is:

- Remove the person from the source of intoxication in case of being inhaled.

• In case of being absorbed, rinse the affected area with plenty of water.

• Remove contaminated clothing with gloves.

• Check if the person is conscious, breathing and has a pulse.

• DO NOT induce vomiting. AND TRANSFER TO THE HOSPITAL.

14.- Basic elements of a first aid kit:

Antiseptics: (cleaning and disinfection)

• Isodine (iodine)

• Alcohol

• Antibacterial soap. Healing material

Instrumental:

• Dextrostix

• Pair of scissors

• Tweezers

• Deaf lamp.

• Thermometer

• Baumanometer

• Lancets Medications:

• Oral serum life packs.

Inside, you'll also discover detailed information on:

1- Basic Definitions.
   - First aid.
2. Personal safety.
   - Evaluation of the scene, security, and situation.
   -Security rules.
3.-Injured evaluation
   -Immediate Simultaneous Evaluation
   -Primary evaluation.
   -Secondary evaluation.
4.-Vital Signs.
   -Technique V.E.S.
   -Normal values of vital signs
5.-Airway obstruction.
   - Manual methods of airway management.
   -Adult airway clearance maneuver.
   -Adult airway clearance maneuver unconscious ....

ISBN 9798546796174

INDISPENSABLE
GUIDE DE LA SANTE
INTESTINALE